The Revd Dr Stephen Orch
Christian Education Moveme
Cambridge Theological Fede
minster College, Cambridge,
The United Reformed Churc
him Moderator for 2007–8.

A HUMAN JESUS
Meditations and Prayers through the Year

Stephen Orchard

First published in Great Britain in 2006

Society for Promoting Christian Knowledge
36 Causton Street
London SW1P 4ST

The prayers in this book were first included in *All the Glorious Names*,
a prayer handbook published by the United Reformed Church.

British Library Cataloguing-in-Publication Data
A catalogue record for this book is available from the British Library.

ISBN-13: 978-0-281-05881-5
ISBN-10: 0-281-05881-4

1 3 5 7 9 10 8 6 4 2

Typeset by Graphicraft Ltd, Hong Kong
Printed in Great Britain by Bookmarque Ltd, Croydon, Surrey

Contents

Part 3
SON OF MAN

Introduction

The book has been prepared in three parts, each directing prayer and meditation towards an aspect of Jesus. It is called *A Human Jesus* not because Christ's divinity is held in question but in order to emphasize how the Jesus who is Lord of all embraces what it is to be human. As one of the meditations suggests, the idea of a human Jesus sounds rather friendly when, in fact, humanity can also be terrifying. The prayers form a thematic cycle, which can be used weekly, though it is equally suited to a daily routine. The first 12 prayers can be used in the weeks before Easter, with the theme 'Jesus, Son of Mary'; the second and third groups, each of 20 prayers, centre on 'Christ, Son of God' and 'Son of Man' respectively, which brings us back to the celebration of the Incarnation. The sequence ends with a final prayer of adoration. Another way of using the prayers is to see them as centring on different aspects of the person of Christ – as the Jesus of history, the risen Lord and the ideal of all humanity. Each prayer is based on a lection. Reading this Bible passage will give the context in which the prayer was written. The prayers are often preceded by a meditation and sometimes followed by a collect.

Stephen Orchard

Part 1

JESUS, SON OF MARY

Give him the name Jesus

Luke 1.26–38

What shall we call the child?
What name shall we give her?
It is hard to give a child the right name
because it will shape a life
and put a mark right into the soul.
It might not be a name she likes when she grows up.
Is it a name our family and friends will like?
What do other people think of a name like that?

Jesus, Joshua, God is salvation.
The Son of the Most High, the mighty and everlasting
    king –
all this for a child not yet conceived,
not yet lying in the manger;
and as we greet the babe with awe and wonder
we lay this great cross upon his shoulders.

Jesus, thank you for living your name,
for taking the role of Saviour to your inmost being,
for living and breathing justice and compassion.
Thank you for your human birth
and your standing beside us in repentance for sins.
Thank you for the searching of the heart in the wilderness
which led you to see what God had called you to do.
Thank you for the miles of road you walked
in search of those who would listen and follow.
Thank you for the anger which blazed against the self-
    righteous,
who thought they knew the way to God

2

but blocked the road for others.
Thank you for wearying yourself in healing the sick
and listening to problem upon problem.
Thank you for feeding the hungry
and sending the rich away empty.
Thank you for your despair and agony,
your suffering and your death.

Now I take to myself the Christian name
by which you know me as your own
and say again that I will follow you,
glad to be in your family and to carry your name.

What do you want with us?

Mark 1.21–8

A human Jesus is always a nice Jesus,
someone who is a discreet and approving friend.
Jesus of Nazareth, the boy next door,
who always puts things in such a charming way
and reads the scriptures so beautifully.
When he tells you something is so then you believe him.
So why introduce this ugly note?
Why listen to the cry of the maniac,
that in this Jesus is to be found the fearful holiness of God,
the fiery purging of our souls to the point of destruction?

Your teaching is most wonderful;
your words make my pulse race faster
and my mind is alert and ready.
I delight in those pithy sentences
which say everything to me at once
yet leave me discovering new richness
as the days and years go by.
I honour their wisdom and insight,
I am humbled by their truth;
yet in my heart of hearts I know that that is not enough;
you want more from me than admiration and delight.
You want to show me that holiness of God
which I fear will blind my eyes.
To really hear your teaching is to open myself to destruction.
Yet you say that truly to understand and follow you
I must trust myself to be broken and re-made.
Admit me as a disciple: let me hear you speak.

We pray for all those who teach in the name of Jesus, that through their lips and lives many may come to ask the question, 'What do you want with us, Jesus of Nazareth?'

Jesus, son of Joseph

John 6.30–51

'Joshua bar Joseph'; even in that form
it leads us to the realization that we mean Jesus
and we all think we know about Jesus.
We know too much to stand beside those Jews
and see how blasphemous it was for them
that one whose parentage was obvious to all
could claim to have come down from heaven.
We know too little to stand beside those Jews
and see with them the need for a prophetic sign,
like bread in the desert, to testify to God's work.

God, you nourish and sustain us
all through our lives.
Each breath of air, each drop of water and each crumb of
*   bread*
comes from your hand.
Your spirit takes the dust and breathes it into life.
You feed our imagination, so that eyes and ears and hands
respond to new sensations every second.
When all our being takes your gifts of every kind
and in our daily life we find one glad wholeness,
a sense that all is right and good because you bless it,
we are most truly fed.

We thank you that the very ordinariness of our being,
our birth and breathing, one among so many,
is drawn, with that of Jesus, son of Joseph,
to the heart of heaven.

Jesus, Son of Mary

When we break bread with thanksgiving
may his presence be with us.
When we recall his words
may we be taught by you.
When we hymn your praise
may we catch the echo of the saints who sing for ever.

Come, Lord Jesus, come quickly.

The Son of Man has nowhere to lay his head
Matthew 8.20

Surely there was a bed waiting in Bethany
or Capernaum or a hundred homes in Galilee
where Jesus was a welcome guest?
Yes, but not a home. It is not just shelter
that the fox finds in his hole
but a place of safety and retreat;
the bird makes a nest for her young
to raise the brood, not just to comfort them.

The nomad Jesus, the man for others,
pays the price, not only in discomfort,
not only in being insecure – with no fixed address –
but of belonging everywhere and nowhere,
his only home with his Father,
who made his home in him.

Follow him to the ends of the earth
and you will find no resting place
except the love and presence of the unseen God.
It may be better to sleep at home
than to face that transformation.

You call me to follow you;
you wait for me at every turn of the road;
you add the spring to my step
and you pace me when the going is hard.
Bear with me when my dragging feet betray,
not that I am tired,

but that my heart is not in the journey
and the kingdom is not my goal.

God of the nomad and the pilgrim, may we find our security in you and not in our possessions. May our homes be open to guests and our hearts to one another so that all our travelling is lighter and together we reach the goal.

I lend him to the Lord

1 Samuel 1.21–8

He was lent. Not just for an hour,
not with an intention to claim him back.
but without limit, for the rest of his life.
Lent, because he was God's gift,
as all children are.
Lent, because the gift was joyfully received
and loved and therefore gladly offered back.
When we, who receive so much,
squirrel away God's gifts against our future needs
will it ever cross our minds to lend them back
with no strings attached?

May the one who was once a child
come again in children
bringing delight and promise.

May the one who was once a child
fill children's lives
with wonder, creativity and love.

May the one who was once a child
save children from misery,
from cruelty, hunger and disease.

May we who are children
grow in knowledge and the love of God.

May we who are adults
nurture and respect all children.

May we who are parents
never confuse love with possession
and care with domination.

May we all prepare children
to love God and their neighbours
in unselfconscious devotion.

God, you give us so many things in answer to our prayers; receive back the unreserved offering of ourselves and all that we have in gratitude and praise.

I will give you peace

2 Samuel 7.1–16

The great king David in his cedar palace
was also the shepherd boy.
The prince over Israel was also the fugitive,
the guerrilla fighter looking for his chance
to stage a coup.

He knew that only God could raise him to the throne,
that only God could turn history round
and overrule his anger, his jealousy and lust,
making him a prince of peace.
His heirs were builders of the Temple
to glorify so marvellous a God.
David, from civil war and broken promises,
brought justice and peace
which was remembered even when the Temple
was looted, violated and wrecked.

Make us citizens of your kingdom, Lord,
and make your home in us.

When the riot sirens fill the night with noise,
when the young men hurl brick-ends
and the young women scream defiance
        show us the way to peace.

When the government forces make another raid
into the mountains where the rebels are hidden
and the homes of the villagers blaze to ashes
        show us the way to peace.

Jesus, Son of Mary

When the pistol is held to the pilot's head
and the passengers cower in their seats
while people bargain with their lives
    show us the way to peace.

When the machine guns rattle across the gullies
and helicopters fire their rockets into the trees
and people stagger in their flight and fall
    show us the way to peace.

Make us citizens of your kingdom, Lord,
and make your home in us.

Jesus, son of Joseph, from Nazareth

John 1.43–51

The Son of God had to be someone's child,
to be brought up and make a living somewhere,
and lay himself open to the cheap joke
about his home and family.
Nazareth! Is it an old mining village
or an area of urban deprivation?
Is it tucked away in rural poverty,
too far for weekend cottages?
Or is it a new town where no one smart lives?
Being the son of Joseph won't open many doors in life,
for his is not one of the better families,
not the kind of start in life to take you to the top,
and not the place to find the Son of God.

Please let me not jump to so many conclusions;
open my eyes to my prejudices,
so that I can allow for them and set them aside.
I have a mind full of stereotypes
filing people by their gender, colour, social class,
their manners, politics and, yes, their faith.
All this impoverishes my life and is unjust;
all this impoverishes the lives of others,
belittling, wronging, making them less human.
I need to come and see, to make a move;
I need to shift the ground of my thinking.
So I ask you to send me friends to move me along;
I ask you to help me even through those I wrong;
I ask it sincerely, being prepared to change my mind.

Like Philip, may we try to open eyes;
like Jesus, may we stand with the despised.

14

We will not kill you

Judges 15.9–17

No, we will not kill you,
but we will hand you over to those who will.
Anything to keep the blood from our hands:
anything to distance ourselves from responsibility.
Let other people take decisions,
especially when we are in a tight corner.
We never laid a finger on the Lord's anointed one,
so let no one say we did.

Are we then surprised that the Cross
looms so large on the world's horizon,
ready for the one who is prepared to make the sacrifice?
The one who lets himself be handed over to death
becomes the only one who wins the victory.

Betrayed Jesus, you know that my faith
cannot always be counted upon.
Mocked Jesus, you know how I have
laughed aside your claims on me.
Scourged Jesus, you know that I have
added to your wounds my heartlessness.
Rejected Jesus, you know that I have clamoured
for the popular choice and not the truth.
Crucified Jesus, you know that I stand
broken-hearted at your Cross,
my integrity shattered and my will broken.

Risen Jesus, you know my need for your forgiveness;
raise my buried hopes that I may serve you.

Jesus, Son of Mary

Ascended Jesus, pour out your spirit upon me
that I may teach and heal in your name.
Eternal Christ, may I sing your praise
with all your people
as you fill the whole earth with your glory.

Alleluia.

Jesus of Nazareth is passing by

Luke 18.35–43

What the blind man heard was the crowd,
the voices, the feet on the road, jingles and swishes,
bringing possible danger and certain bewilderment.
They told him it was Jesus of Nazareth,
but he shouted 'Jesus, Son of David'.
Not a Nazarene but from Bethlehem in Judaea:
not a Galilean, virtually a Gentile,
but of the house and lineage of David.
He could see, or he could sense,
that it was worth seeking Jesus's interest
and crying for his pity.

If only I could see.
If only I could make the connections.
Son of David, have pity on me.

Jesus, borne along by crowds of suppliants
you still hear the single voice that calls,
have pity on me.
You, involved in a world of need,
fill every desperate heart with hope,
and each life with new meaning.

Help us to see that in your vulnerability
there is strength; in your compassion, fire;
and in your openness a rock.
Help us to see your kingdom close at hand,
hidden in space and time, but always there.
Help us to see that all things are being healed,

even when some look broken and destroyed.
For when we walk by faith, and not by sight,
gratitude fills our being.
We shout and sing your praise;
the vision lifts our spirits,
until we are overwhelmed with joy.

Hosanna, peace, glory to God.

With Jesus the Galilean
Matthew 26.69–75

So he was notorious, then, this Jesus;
one of those people to avoid.
Perhaps it was the message,
or just the provincialism and the accent;
well, we only believe those who are like us –
who wants to be different? Then, suddenly,
it is not a question of taste or fashion
but of life or death,
whether we belong with this Jesus.

Lord, remember me when you come to your kingdom
even though I forget you;
remember me, even when I deny you.

Lord, remember me when the days flow by and fill them-
selves with things that do not matter and only distract
me from following your way.
Lord, remember me when I find it convenient to keep the
light under the bucket rather than on the stand because
I don't want to draw attention to myself.
Lord, remember me when I distance myself from you in case
there are embarrassing questions.
Lord, remember me when I send you back to Galilee and
say that your friendship counts for nothing today.
Lord, remember me when all I say and do denies everything
for which you stood and died, when my whole life
testifies 'I do not know the man'.

Lord, remember me . . .

Most gracious God, you made us, you mend us and, in your own good time, you perfect us. Look kindly on all those who find it impossible to declare their Christian faith openly, especially those who stand in fear of their lives. Call them once more to share in nourishing your people and leading your Church. Turn their weeping into joy and their fears into stronger faith; for the sake of Jesus.

Obedience is better than sacrifice

1 Samuel 15.17–30

That is a hard doctrine,
hard on us and very hard on the Amalekites.
Polytheism would be so much easier;
they could have their gods and we could have ours.
Nice liberal people are happier with polytheism,
because then God, who is our splendour,
is not in control when terrible things happen.
Anarchy is better than a god who allows a holocaust, or
   is it?
Or perhaps we could have a god who changes his mind,
who is capricious, one day slaughtering – another,
   forgiving.
But the God who counts our obedience more important
than the offerings we make to buy him off
is not afraid to be obedient and to offer himself in real
   sacrifice.

Lord, you teach me many hard lessons in life
and I cannot believe you are in control
when I see and experience pain and injustice.
Must it always be so costly to put things right?
You set before me Jesus, walking a narrow road of obedience,
which cost him everything; and still you call, Follow me,
take this cup, whoever wants to save their life must lose it.
Why do you ask this of me?
Why can't your reign of justice and peace simply come?
Why does it all have to be at a price?
You ask of me obedience and not questions,
yet Jesus asked those questions of you in Gethsemane,

and, as his disciple, I must ask them too.
Strengthen me to hear the answers;
strengthen all those who bear and suffer in their discipleship.
Renew our compassion, but also our determination
never to temporize with evil
or stop struggling for your justice.

The son of Mary

Mark 6.1–6

'A fine family this Mary has,
a woman can be proud of five sons
and all those useful daughters.
A pity about Jesus.
What a disappointment he must be to her
after he promised so well.'
'All those fine words and he can do nothing for us,
her neighbours and friends.'
'What can she think of him?'

My deepest being praises God,
my inmost heart is transformed with joy
because I know that God is my saviour.
God looks at me with such loving eyes
although I am only the lowest servant.

From this moment it will be clear to all
that I have been marvellously blessed
and that God has recognized me as his child.
Every succeeding generation will know
that the mighty One has transformed my life beyond
   imagining.
The only name for God is 'the One who is holy'.

The One whose mercy can be relied upon
by those who keep faith
as the centuries of history roll by.
The One whose greatness is revealed in action.
The One who roots out arrogance,

exposes rulers to judgement
and gives power to the unassuming.
The One who prepares a feast for the hungry
and turns away the rich at the door.

This is my God, who stands by us all
and whose mercy will long outlast us.

Praise to the Holy One.

Part 2
CHRIST, SON OF GOD

Captives in Christ's triumphal procession
2 Corinthians 2.12–17

Those ancient generals, celebrating triumphs, led their victims and their booty through the streets to demonstrate their power. It was a glorious victory for those who rode alongside the conqueror; and it was a terrible humiliation if you dragged your feet with the slaves. Yet we, who are Christians, choose to walk as captives because we trust the conqueror and applaud his way of winning victory.

Because I believe in the power of the Cross,
in service and sacrifice, in love and obedience,
as the only weapons for fighting evil,

I will follow your lead and offer my service.

Because I believe in Resurrection power
which makes the withered stems blossom,
the dead ends turn into broad roads
and the lost cause become a victory,

I will follow your lead and offer my service.

Because I believe in the power of the Holy Spirit
making what is obscure plain,
turning weakness to strength,
and giving shape and meaning to my hopes,

I will follow your lead and offer my service.

Christ, Son of God

Most glorious Christ, you have taken power to yourself through love and sacrifice; take us as your subjects so that we may be free citizens of your kingdom.

I now believe

John 11.21–7

Can this really be Martha?
Is this the woman too busy with the house
to sit and learn at the feet of Jesus?
Surely only the attentive disciple,
only the earnest student of the rabbi,
can reach that certainty of faith
which trusts the word before the deed?
Many were converted after Lazarus was raised.
Martha, 'the practical one', believed before.

We pray for those impatient with words,
the activists who have had enough of talking
and want to see something done.

May Christ bring them time to reflect.

We pray for those broken by grief,
who have watched over the beds of the dying
and feel that they have failed in love
and fill their lives with vain regret.

May Christ lift them from despair.

We pray for those who are looking for certainties that they
    will never find;
who cannot accept the assurances of faith,
nor build on their experience of love
but go on, anxious and doubting,
searching for the proof to end all proofs.

Christ, Son of God

May Christ call them from the tomb.

We give thanks for the witnesses to faith,
for the Marys and the Marthas, the Peters and the
    Thomases,
who have come to put their trust in Christ,
not only in the past, but now.

May Christ unite us in his risen power.

For to me to live is Christ

Philippians 1.19–26

It is all very well for the apostle,
for a holy man like Paul,
to say that for him life is Christ.
It is all very well for him
to hope that Christ will shine out in his person,
whether he lives or dies.
How can I live with that intensity?
How can I face even death with hope
and fill my life with holiness?

When somewhere above the street lamps
I can see the brightening of the sky
which means another day is dawning,
        may Christ revive my spirit.

When in the crowded bus,
among the jostling cars on the motorway
and the airless morning train,
I see the human faces of the travellers,
        may Christ be found beside me.

When the routine of work is numbing,
when anxiety turns to anger
and my patience is exhausted,
        may Christ be my fellow-worker.

When I hurry through another meal
without a time to savour and digest

and hurry on to fill my night with business,
may Christ nourish me.

When the television images flicker before me,
half-watched, forgotten in a moment,
even when they picture what I need to know,
may Christ open my eyes.

Christ before, behind and with me.
Christ in every word and every experience.
Christ in the friend and stranger.
Christ in transforming happiness or pain.
Our full humanity is found in him.

God's secret

Colossians 1.24—2.5

Some people like a mystery,
like to know something others don't know
and like to keep it to themselves.
Some people keep a secret
because they dare not tell it;
they are terrified of being found out.
Some people have secrets
which they intend to share
but they are waiting for the right time.
We like our secrets, they make us important
and we keep or tell them with that in mind.

Even now, someone is keeping a secret
nagging away in their mind
and blocking the road forward;
  may they find a forgiving ear.

Even now, someone is keeping a secret
that would make the lives of others easier,
but they would rather keep it quiet;
  may they break out of their selfishness.

Even now, someone is preparing someone else
to hear a secret hard to bear
because it brings pain and heartbreak;
  may their love be strengthened.

Even now, someone is teaching
and opening a storehouse of secrets

to enrich the lives of others;
       may they learn together.

Even now, someone is being let into a secret,
that open secret, which still needs to be spoken,
the secret which is Christ Jesus;
       may they with us become a sign of hope.

By day a pillar of cloud . . .
by night a pillar of fire

Exodus 13.17–22

God, urgent and fleeting,
God, pulling people on,
giving no rest until the goal is reached.
God, not even letting the buried bones rest,
but still calling us forward.
God, anticipating our fear
and drawing us on from everything that enslaves us.

You have yourself become the sign,
the drifting cloud along the horizon,
the shaft of light in the dark night,
the teacher from Nazareth.

How shall we keep pace with you?
We want to pin you down,
like a specimen we have caught,
so that we can describe
exactly what you are like
and everything about your nature;
    forgive our limited imagination.

We want to hold you back,
dragging on the hand which pulls forward,
shouting, 'No further, no further!
We have trod the road too far';
    forgive our stubbornness.

We want to close our eyes
in case we see where you are leading,

letting the cloud drift on
and the light dance away;
> *forgive our blindness.*

You would not call us
> *unless the journey were worth making.*
You would not go before
> *unless the goal were worthwhile.*
We can rely on your promise,
> *and we are coming as fast as we can.*

He has put all things under his feet
Ephesians 1.15–23

All things, not just the Church, but all things under his
    feet.
Everything that seems so powerful,
so terrible that we cannot resist it,
so influential that there is nothing we can do;
all these mighty things are heaped together
under the feet of Christ like so many old cushions.
Above any government and sovereignty,
above the riot police and the tanks,
above vested interest and corruption,
above political establishments,
above all things the reign of Christ.

Lord, we were going to do something about poverty,
about hunger, ignorance and disease,
but it was all too much for us,
beyond our giving or our understanding.

Lord, we were going to do something about violence,
about the arms race, nuclear weapons
and those who make a profit out of war,
but we couldn't make sense of it
and we couldn't see what we should do.

Lord, we were going to do something about ecology,
about the disappearance of the forests,
the rare species and the irreplaceable plants,
but it really is very difficult
and none of us are expert in these matters.

Christic, Son of God

Lord, we are good at learning a little
and wringing our hands in helplessness.
We believe we need to know a great deal more
so that we can put our backs into it.
We need to take the power you have given
and set about claiming our inheritance.
Fill your Church and every one of us
with your fullness, authority and love,
so that everything may be redeemed and brought to unity
    in Christ.

The Spirit of truth

John 16.12–15

Come, Holy Spirit, and show us what is true.

In a world of great wealth
where many go hungry
and fortunes are won and lost
by trading in money,
    come, Holy Spirit, and show us what is true.

In a world of great knowledge
where many die in ignorance
and every piece of information
has a price in the market place,
    come, Holy Spirit, and show us what is true.

In a world of easy communication,
where words leap between continents
and we expect to see a picture
to illustrate each item of the news,
    come, Holy Spirit, and show us what is true.

In a Church which speaks a thousand accents,
divided over doctrine, creed and ministry,
more anxious for itself than for the Gospel,
    come, Holy Spirit, and show us what is true.

In a Church touched by the flame of Pentecost,
moved to generous sacrifice and costly love,
interpreting the will of God with new insight,
    come, Holy Spirit, and show us what is true.

Creator Spirit, move in all our hearts,
giving us new insight into the mysteries of God
and a new determination to live by the Gospel
so that we, with all humanity, may find our unity in Christ.

Not a matter of talk, but of power

1 Corinthians 4.14–21

Given the choice, most of us
would rather the apostle came in love
and in a gentle spirit, than with a rod.
Most of us find Paul's *words*
quite enough to remind us of his zeal.
Until, that is, the self-important run the church
and bend us to their purposes
to build up their own self-esteem
and not the service of Christ;
then we would like a strong apostle
to put everything in order
and turn blustering to kingdom power.

When we sit down in committee, Lord,
remind us it's not talk but power,
not endless analysis but action plans we need.
Not the will of the eloquent but your will be done.

When we visit our neighbour in distress
remind us it's not talk but power,
not explaining everything to them
but offering the loving action beyond words.

When we set out on your mission to the world
in the humdrum places where it all begins
remind us it's not talk but power,
and help us to transform the world,
not bore it to death with preaching.

Christ, Son of God

When we come together in worship
remind us it's not talk but power;
stop us sermon tasting and prayer testing
as if the length and breadth were everything
and the simple and the silent had no power.

Remind us in the fullness of your love
that power, not talk, is the stuff of your kingdom.
Remind us, or else the harsher discipline
of seeing the kingdom slipping from us
will fill us with remorse.
Remind us in the fullness of your love.

Lost to sight

1 Thessalonians 2.17—3.10

How would Paul keep his churches in sight today?
How, with so many millions of Christians,
speaking so many hundred languages,
can anyone keep them all in sight?
Some are isolated by repression,
some by poor communications, some by choice.
All are held together in the unity of Christ
but how shall we live and pray that unity?

*We pray for the Christians who meet in fear, because the laws
of their country forbid worship
or allow it only on sufferance; for those forbidden to teach
their children
or to tell the good news to their neighbours.*

*We pray for the Christians in the minority in cultures
which are at odds with their faith: who withdraw into
the safety of the Church rather than live in dialogue with
others.*

*We pray for the Christians in the majority, whose churches
lead the nation and occupy positions of privilege, with all
the temptations which that brings.*

*We pray for the Christians we shall never know, because the
accidents of history keep from us the details of their witness and their lives; may the Spirit unite us in purpose
and hope.*

We pray for ourselves as unknown Christians, not at the centre of the Church, but on the rim when seen from other countries, other churches. May we find the grace to learn from others and the humility to know our own shortcomings.

We rejoice in the life and witness of the churches lost to sight from our point of view, but held together in the body of Christ Jesus our Lord.

Jacob then blessed Pharaoh

Genesis 47.1–12

The story of Israel in Egypt is not all plagues,
not all a desperate rush of escaping slaves.
Two nations with different cultures
and very different faiths
can live in prosperity and mutual respect.
The empty-handed refugees from famine
have human dignity and human skills.
The powerful and prosperous can be generous
and Israel's future be secured by the Egyptians.

When the hungry refugees leave home
and strike out into unknown territory
in their search for food and security
         may God give them a compassionate welcome.

When the reception camps are bursting at the seams
and broken people are dying of despair
because they see no end to their sufferings
         may God turn compassion to commitment.

When resettlement programmes bring people
to strange houses in foreign towns
where no one speaks their language
         may God find them true friends.

When citizens are taunted for their colour,
their houses burned, their children beaten

and the blame for all the nation's ills
laid at their door
> *may God bring them justice.*

May Jesus Christ, who once fled as a helpless refugee, be the friend and protector of those making a new life in a strange land, and of their children and their children's children.

I will not let Israel go

Exodus 5

People do not give up power or economic advantage on
    request;
they cling to it,
just as we cling to our possessions,
to our homes and to our lifestyle.
When it seemed their way of life was threatened
the Egyptians practised a little firm government,
making the people work harder for their living,
reducing the time they had for revolution,
and discrediting agitators like Moses.

Christ, you ask us for love and justice.
and so we pray for people held as slaves,
people bought and sold as commodities,
chosen without a right to choose.
> *They are our brothers and sisters*
> *and we will work for their good.*

Christ, you ask us for love and justice,
and so we pray for underpaid people, selling their labour cheap
because they have no choice of job
and need the work to make a living.
> *They are our brothers and sisters*
> *and we will work for their good.*

Christ, you ask us for love and justice,
and so we pray for powerful people living on the backs of
*   the poor,*

whose wealth is infected with the plagues of injustice and
*   fear.*
*   They are our brothers and sisters*
*   and we will work for their good.*

Christ, you ask us for love and justice,
and so we pray for ourselves.
Open our eyes to our own role as exploiters of the weak
and our hearts to the poor on our own doorstep.
*   They are our brothers and sisters*
*   and they are working for our good.*

I am at my wits' end about you
Galatians 4.12–20

Sometimes the child exasperates the parent and sometimes
    the parent the child.
Sometimes the minister exasperates the congregation
and sometimes the congregation the minister.
Sometimes the Christian cries 'no more'
because the mission seems impossible
and the world oblivious to the truth.
To bring up children is a patient task;
done well, it may bring heartbreak.

*We pray for stipendiary ministers. May they discharge their
duties faithfully and have a high sense of the privilege which
is theirs. When the local church is mean and insensitive
may they not be discouraged; when their fellow members
are considerate may they not take unfair advantage.*

*We pray for non-stipendiary ministers. May they take the
opportunities which are theirs to renew the ministry of
the Church imaginatively. When the churches fail to use
them may their sense of calling be renewed; when they
are challenged beyond their strength may they find sup-
port and encouragement.*

*We pray for ministers who are long retired and find their
ministry in prayer and private counsel with their visitors.
May they not become bitter with vain regret about their
failing powers; may we appreciate their present ministry
and give them the dignity which is theirs.*

Holy Spirit, giver of life,
you have poured out gifts among us,
you have brought joy as we serve you,
you have given strength and courage for our weakness;
from you we have received grace upon grace.
Shape all of us in the fellowship of your Church
to be a holy and dedicated people, now and for ever.

No longer a slave but an heir

Galatians 4.1–11

Why don't we live as free people?
Why do we expect 'them' to tell us what to do?
The people at 'headquarters', the bishops,
the ministers, the deacons, the committee –
the people who tell us what to do.
We expect it and resent it.
We do not see them as friends and colleagues
but as directors or rivals.

Help us to live as heirs of the kingdom.
We worship in small groups in big cities,
our voices echoing in empty galleries.
We gather in twos and threes in little country churches,
in bedsitters and spare rooms;
help us to live as heirs of the kingdom.

We worship in large groups in suburbs
with our cars parked beneath the trees.
We worship in busy towns
in chapels of historic importance.
We worship in great rallies
raising a thousand hearts in praise;
help us to live as heirs of the kingdom.

You have called us to witness and service,
wherever we are gathered.
You have given us leaders, to help us
worship, witness and serve to your glory.
Help us to live together as heirs of the kingdom.

Christ, Son of God

Deliver us from self-seeking leadership
which sacrifices your Church to personal vanity.
Deliver us from expecting too much
of leaders who are too willing for our good.
May we use the gift of leadership in others
to the glory of your Church.
May we discover gifts of leadership in ourselves
so that we may live as heirs of the kingdom.

Bethel

Genesis 35.6–20

The place where God had spoken with Jacob,
this God who creates nations
and intervenes in family feuds;
this God who is at births and deaths
and whose presence is remembered
by marking out some places as sacred.
Bethel is recreated around the world
and the Bethlehem road travelled
by new tribes of pilgrims.

God of my weeping, meet me
when those I love are lost to me,
and the tears well up
and I do not know where to turn;
when life has lost its focus
and I am hurt deep within myself,
meet me in the loneliness and pain,
giving it meaning and reassuring me
so that I may set up a pillar
reminding me of your goodness.

God of my laughter, meet me
when I cannot believe my good fortune,
when the whole world is sunny,
full of friends and happiness,
my future secure, my gifts employed,
and I feel loved and wanted,
meet me in the joy and success
giving it meaning and challenging me,

so that I may set up a pillar
reminding me of your goodness.

Without you I have no identity,
no real name or purpose for my life.
You have met with us all in Bethlehem.
May my pillars mark the way there.

Experts in goodness but simpletons in evil

Romans 16.16–20

How could I be so naive? What was I thinking of
to let myself be talked into walking the extra mile
and giving away my coat? How can the Church survive
if it keeps on pouring itself out for others?
Someone has to draw the line
so that the funds are safeguarded and the doctrine pure!
Someone has to fight for the truth and proper moral
    standards
if evil is to be defeated!

> *God of peace, give us grace to defeat evil.*

When we are caught up in quarrels
that split churches and break friendships,
when our blood pressure rises
and our mouths are dry with anger
> *God of peace, give us grace to defeat evil.*

When we are carried along by eloquence
so that we come to believe
that what suits us is always right
and what is immediately obvious is your will
> *God of peace, give us grace to defeat evil.*

When we cannot understand
why people should be so wicked
and we are tempted to throw away
our tolerance and our charity
in case they are abused,
> *God of peace, give us grace to defeat evil.*

Teach us the gracious way to give moral leadership,
the liberating way to help other people,
and the generous way to live our lives,
so that we may learn to be experts in the goodness
which is stronger than all the powers of evil,
because of Christ Jesus our Lord.

He is your praise

Deuteronomy 10.12–22

Praise God, who has set bounds to the universe,
and brought each one of us to birth,
who has been at work in our history
and in every living thing.

Praise God, whose will is justice and love,
who marks out no one for privilege
and whose favours cannot be bought.

Praise God, who redresses the balance
in favour of the defenceless and the poor,
and calls on us to do the same.

Praise God, who loves the foreigner
and finds a home for the stranger
and reminds us that we have been outsiders.

Praise God, who has brought us happiness
and looks only for humility in return,
for wondering minds and thankful hearts.

We stand in awe of you, our God;
your thoughts are beyond our understanding
and your love puts us to shame.

We hear your commandments, our God,
and ask your forgiveness
because we have fallen so far short
of the love for you and the generosity
which you ask us to show to others.

Christ, Son of God

We offer ourselves in your service, our God,
wholeheartedly and without condition.
Whatever merit we have comes from you,
all that is worthwhile bears your stamp.
For you are our praise, our voice, our being.

As far round as Illyricum

Romans 15.14–24

There was the Paul of Rome and Corinth,
Jerusalem, Antioch, Ephesus
and all the fleshpots of the ancient world:
and then there was the Paul
who travelled country roads and turned aside
to find the places no one else had visited,
because it was important to see them too
and share his vision.

God of the lonely country,
the great bare fields and bricked-up farms,
the derelict railway and the weekly bus,
the empty weekend cottage
in the old school or post office,
*   remember us.*

God of the lonely country,
where jobs are hard to find,
the wages low and the prices high,
where the young go off to the city
and the old come back to retire,
*   remember us.*

God of the lonely country
which can be so beautiful,
so beautiful to see but harsh for living,
you care for everything and everyone
throughout your marvellous creation;
*   remember us.*

60

Christ, Son of God

God of the back road and solitary cottage,
beside the single worker in the hedgeless plain
and the single worker in the rural kitchen;
God of the many miles between a home
and a shop, a school, a church, a friend,
> *remember us all in town and country*

and remind us that we need each other.

Conform to my institutions

Leviticus 18.1–5

Are we not creatures of our time?
Are we not shaped by our history
so that we cannot escape our culture?
Our birth gives us colour, country, language,
perhaps it even gives us faith.
What real freedom do we have?
God asks that we do not conform
to the past that we have known or inherited
but to the future to which he brings us today,
through his laws and institutions.
Our freedom lies within those boundaries.

God of history, we thank you
for the richness of the past
and all that we have learnt from it.
Teach us not to be its slaves,
not to be bound by tradition
but gratefully to look back on it
as a place where we once lived
and from which we have moved.

God of the future, we thank you
for the promise of tomorrow
and the bright horizons of hope.
Save us from living a fantasy
which makes us lean too much
on what might be and not what is.

Christel, Son of God

God of the present, we thank you
for meeting us in every moment,
challenging us to live now
in obedience to your will.
Give us that rich living and fulfilment
which comes from meeting the 'I am'
and offering our lives today in obedience.

... *study the scriptures diligently* ...
John 5.31–40

It is easy to see the error of the Pharisees;
it is always easier to see other people's errors
rather than our own, and more comfortable.
Yet perhaps we will never make their mistake
of missing the Christ in our diligent studies
because we are not diligent students.
How is the Word to find a home in us?

We come to you for life,
to you who first come to us.
We come by roundabout routes
of our own choosing,
ignoring some of the signposts
and criticizing some of the other travellers.
Sometimes we are impatient with the difficulties
and make a dash down the short-cut
which seems so obvious but leads nowhere.
Sometimes we are diverted by the gurus
who seem so plausible at the time.
Again and again we find pleasant places
to halt beside the road and take a rest
and lose time on our way.

You have taught us how to travel,
you have pioneered the way
and left all necessary help.
Become also our travelling companion.
We know that we must bring to the journey
our study and our diligence,

our knowledge and our will.
We dedicate our whole selves
to the task of patient travelling
to the end of the journey
which is with you and to you.

I will ask questions, and you shall answer
Job 40.1–14

So many people ask questions about God,
so many people ask questions beginning with an 'if'.
If God loves us, why suffering?
If God controls, why war?
If God exists, what is the evidence?

So few people turn the questions round
and wonder what God might ask them.
Given love, why do you hate?
Given peace, why do you wreck it?
Given meaning, why do you choose chaos?

Before your greatness, God, I can only be silent.
I keep my mouth tight shut because there is nothing I can say.

Meet me in the depths of my soul and ask your questions of
*   me,*
the questions that I cannot answer because I know so little.

Meet me in that numbing despair
which finds no meaning nor purpose in life.
Meet me in my bewilderment
when nothing makes sense any more.
Meet me in the faithlessness
which doubts your purpose and your love.

Ask your questions of me then,
ask them gently but insistently,
like the constant friend

Christ, Son of God

whose arm around my slumped shoulders
reassures me more than words.
Lift me from despair that narrows my vision
until I stand erect and gaze into your future,
in confidence that nothing can separate me from your love,
and ready to take my share of the task
you are asking all your people to complete.

Part 3

SON OF MAN

A sabbatical

Luke 6.1–11

It is hard for us to grasp as we load the car,
or board the train or aircraft, for a holiday
which takes us miles from home,
that we have lost the meaning of our language
and that for many centuries only 'holy days'
allowed a break from labour.

We, who are rich and privileged,
thank you for the gift of leisure,
for time to unwind, reflect and plan,
to exercise or simply sit in quiet.

We thank you for the people who create our holiday
by working in the cockpit and control-room,
in garage and harbour office;
for those in kitchens, dining rooms and bars,
those guiding tours and running sports and games;
may they too find time for rest and recreation.

We pray for countries where tourism
exaggerates the gap between rich and poor,
distorts the economy and exploits cheap labour;
where gambling and prostitution destroy
all chance of real fulfilment and wealth
for individuals and for nations.

We pray for ourselves as travelling holidaymakers;
may we accept with grace all kindnesses,
as guests and strangers who wish to savour

the rich variety of your good earth.
May we be truly recreated in our recreation,
our lives enlarged with new enthusiasm
and a broader vision of your purpose.

Lord of the Sabbath, teach us to enrich our rest and leisure with reverence and with praise.

Camels and ships

Isaiah 60.1–9

Even in the desert the camel has given way
to the less romantic four-wheel-drive truck
and the ships with sails like doves
have given way to bulk carriers and aircraft.
Yet our commerce and our transport
have all the practicality and excitement
of the desert caravan and sailing dhow.

We pray for the people who design and build our roads,
keeping our safety and convenience in mind. Give them
foresight and imagination in balancing different needs.
May they take pride in their work, especially when the
going is hard.

We pray for the people who manage systems of public trans-
port, often criticized and rarely thanked. May they use
their resources wisely for the benefit of all and maintain
the highest standards of safety and comfort.

We pray for seafarers and air-crew who face unforeseeable
dangers on their journeys and need to be vigilant at all
times. May they return safely to harbour and airport, speed-
ing the trade and friendship of the world.

We pray for maintenance crews and safety teams, whose work
is unseen and unsung until the point of crisis. May they
work to the highest standards with the well-being of all
travellers in their minds.

Son of Man

We pray for ourselves as drivers and passengers, too easily made selfish by anxiety. May we bring patience and skill to our travelling.

As a weaned child

Psalm 131

It could be false modesty
and the burying of talents that keeps us
from busying ourselves with great matters;
it could be a naive trust in authorities,
which allows other people to take decisions
regardless of the consequence.
It could be true humility and the fear of God,
which measures the reality of our lives,
uses our strengths and recognizes our weaknesses.

Teach me to measure myself,
to take a proper account of who I am
and what I have to give.

Where I have been full of self-importance
and lost the chance of offered help,
may I have the grace to apologize.

Where I have busied myself foolishly
with things I never really understood
and set myself up as an expert
when really I am only a beginner,
may I have the wisdom to own up.

Where I have hidden my talent
and not shared the fullness of your gifts in me,
may I set aside shyness and diffidence
and offer myself for the work in hand.

Teach me to measure myself,
to take a proper account of who I am
and what I have to give.

God, I cling to you as a child clings to its mother. Because I want to learn from you and I want to grow to maturity, include me in your family, through Jesus Christ.

Her hope was lost

Ezekiel 19

Can a mother learn to bear the loss of one child
by letting another take its place?
To lose that one as well must be desolation.
Can a mother bear the blighting of her child
if she feels a recovery is possible?
Wasting disease mocks such hope.
What is the cost to God to lose children
by their own folly and faithlessness?

We forget that we are dust;
we have taken pride in our own strength,
believed our wisdom provided all the answers,
trusted our love to last eternally,
only to find that we were weak and foolish
and full of hate.
    Forgive us and remake us.

We forget that we are dust;
we have made our plans and thought our dreams
were on the point of realization,
only to taste the bitterness of failure
and the scorn of those who thought us foolish.
    Forgive us and remake us.

We forget that we are dust;
we traded on your mercy as we wronged each other
and sought cheap grace to patch things up,
only to fall deeper into hate and war
and drag others into misery and death.
    Forgive us and remake us.

Son of Man

You joined us in the dust,
you bore within yourself both the pain of failure
and all that grief which breaks the human will
and stops us loving as the world turns sour;
share with us the forgiveness
which comes from the heart of your desolation.

No water there

Jeremiah 14.1–6

The life of even the strongest is very fragile,
dependent on the elements and the human impulses
of every other living soul.

I have taken your rain for granted;
I have taken it for granted that rain will fall,
the reservoirs and wells will fill,
the pumpers and the purifiers do their work
and water pour out from the kitchen tap.
I have taken your rain for granted.

I have taken your earth for granted;
I have taken it for granted that coal will be dug
and oil and gas piped across continents,
atomic power be harnessed, winds and tides
be turned to good account, to give me energy,
to heat and power my home and run my car;
I have taken your earth for granted.

I have taken people for granted;
I have taken it for granted that people
will want to love and care for each other
and feel they have a duty to the poor and weak,
to nourish children and to nurse the sick;
I have taken people for granted.

God of power and love, I stand in awe of your
creation in all its complexity. Renew that sense
of worship in us all and our sense of mutual

obligation. Reaffirm the vocation of all who work
in public services and utilities to serve the
common good. Forgive my self-centredness and call
us all into your new community in Jesus Christ.

Waste

Isaiah 34.8–15

Not only in ancient ruined cities
but in and around the modern city
are the waste-heaps and garbage of our lives,
picked over by the foxes and the crows
and the human scavengers who make a living there.

Forgive us, Lord, for mentioning
our rubbish in our prayers.
We would rather enjoy the fruits of creation
and forget about the consequences.
Forgive us our polluted water,
our toxic soil and sulphurous air.
Forgive us all the dumped surpluses,
the slag heaps and the piles of scrap.

We thank you for the signs of your forgiveness;
for the plants and trees which colonize
even the most unsightly ground;
for the animals and birds who learn to live
in secret places in our urban sprawl
and turn our rubbish to good account.

We thank you for those who deal with our rubbish,
who keep our streets and houses healthy;
who guard us against poisons and radiation,
or who turn our waste into new riches.

We pray for those for whom the rubbish tip
is the only source of food and wealth,

picking through others' leavings in the search
to keep their family alive.

Most generous giver, from whose creation
there is enough for all and to spare,
make us wise stewards of the earth's treasure
and generous in our turn to one another.

They all ate to their hearts' content
Mark 8.1–10

We thank you for our food;
for the table laden for a celebration
with the rich harvest of your earth;
for the plates and dishes brimming over.
We thank you for our food.

We thank you for our food;
for the bread and cheese by the road-side
and the hurried snack on a journey;
for the meal-break in the working day.
We thank you for our food.

We thank you for our food;
the colour and texture of ingredients,
the tang of herbs and the smell of spices,
the satisfaction of preparing a tasty meal.
We thank you for our food.

We thank you for our hunger;
for the anticipation of a meal to end the day,
for the work which increases our appetite
and our sense of taste and savour.
We thank you for our hunger.

Lord Jesus Christ, you knew hunger and thirst and
you fed the souls and bodies of those who came to
you in Galilee; give us food and friends to share
it at our tables day by day; share with us your
concern for the unfed; and unite all who break
bread at your table in your company.

The hidden riches of the earth

Job 28.1–12

For the people who mine the depths of earth,
who drill the sea-bed and the desert,
the snow-filled wastes and lonely mountains,
we give you thanks and ask your blessing.

For the people who tend the forge and furnace,
who roll the steel and blow the glass,
who toss hot ingots and beat the metal,
we give you thanks and ask your blessing.

For the people who mill and turn and polish,
who cut the die and shape the mould,
who draw up blueprints, plan production,
we give you thanks and ask your blessing.

For the people who solder and assemble,
and check the microelectronic part,
for those with spanner, gauge and meter,
we give you thanks and ask your blessing.

For the people who saw and plane and sand,
who glue the joints and drive the screws,
who paint and varnish, stain and lacquer,
we give you thanks and ask your blessing.

For the people who monitor the cash-flow,
raise the invoice, pack the goods,
for managers and forward-planners,
we give you thanks and ask your blessing.

Creator God, you have given us so many possibilities of shaping the raw materials of earth for our use and pleasure; may they be a blessing to us and not a curse because of our misuse of them. Teach us to manage them wisely, for our own fulfilment and the benefit of succeeding generations.

Wealth and splendour

Revelation 21.22–7

The great city lit by the glory of God,
the great community gathered from the whole earth,
the place of ultimate holiness and truth
is a place of wealth and splendour;
wealth freed from greed and speculation
to enrich every nation of the earth.

Where the brokers sit at their telephones
and screens flicker with changing prices
        let holiness and truth be found.
Where bankers sit in stuffy rooms
determining the credit of whole nations
        let holiness and truth be found.

Where those with private information
play the system for their own gain
        let holiness and truth begin.
Where individuals store up for themselves
the wealth that belongs to their nation
        let holiness and truth begin.
Where people cheat the tax system
or pay their workers less than their due
        let holiness and truth begin.

Where those with economic skills
share them to bring prosperity for all
        let holiness and truth increase.
Where individuals sacrifice their own wealth

in order to benefit their neighbours
let holiness and truth increase.
Where people work in public service
for modest pay to serve the needy
let holiness and truth increase.

God in whom all riches are found, teach us to live in peace and prosperity throughout the earth.

Worthy is the Lamb, the Lamb that was slain

Revelation 5

The Lamb is also a Lion of Judah,
a brave and conquering lion
leading a victory procession.

The Lamb has seven horns and eyes,
the sign of the all-seeing spirit of God.

But above all the Lamb was slaughtered
and bears upon his body the marks of sacrifice.

Eternal God, let our voices join the song of praise,
let our lips shape your name
and our breath speak amen
to that great chorus of all that lives
in earth and heaven and sings your glory.

Eternal God, open the doors to heaven for us
that we may glimpse what lies beyond words,
the mystery of your power in Christ
to shape all human history.

Creator, Saviour, Prophet of a future
in which we are all reconciled
and share with you the wealth and wisdom
which is your gift to all humanity,
we promise to begin to live like that.

We claim the privileges of our royal priesthood
and take up our responsibilities.

Son of Man

We will praise you in and out of season.
We will serve you in everything we do.
The extra mile will be walked and the cheek will be turned.

We will share your good news in everything we say.
We will be your interpreters
so that the vision of the Lamb – so distant, so difficult –
will be the clear message of hope we share
with a lost and weeping world.

Is this your busy city?

Isaiah 23.1–7

Only the stones remain of those great cities of the Bible.
Even as the prophets spoke
places which were a byword for prosperity
were faced with ruin in war or from disaster.
Our cities also pass their prime
without such drama but with great changes
in the places where we make our living.

For the people who tomorrow will find they are being made
*   redundant and those who must tell them*
*   we ask God's mercy.*

For the people who have spent many weeks unemployed and
*   have lost hope that they will ever have a job again*
*   we ask God's mercy.*

For the people who have trained for jobs they cannot find
*   and who have never known the dignity of being employed*
*   we ask God's mercy.*

For the people dependent on social security payments and
*   the charity of others and those who administer benefit*
*   systems*
*   we ask God's mercy.*

For the people living in neighbourhoods where almost no
*   one earns a wage and those who teach and manage and*
*   police there*
*   we ask God's mercy.*

For those who wring their hands at unemployment but do nothing about it and those who make a profit from the poverty of others
  we ask God's mercy.

Dance, O earth

Psalm 114

Perhaps we cannot dance in worship
because we have so little to dance about;
perhaps we have no cause for thanks,
no marvellous escape from captivity.
But some people are being set free;
some people finding health and sight,
some turning their skills to good account,
so let us dance with them
and celebrate the goodness of God.

Wells are springing in the desert
and new shoots push out of the watered earth;
the land responds to human labour
and yields its harvest:
> *let the people dance.*

Stone by stone they pile up a dam
which the rains fill with sweet water;
the animals graze contentedly
and children play around the fields;
> *let the people dance.*

The craft-workers shape storage baskets,
weave patterned cloth and beat metal;
the potters stroke the clay into jars
and the old people tend the fire;
> *let the people dance.*

The rich people in the cities are learning
that they must care for each other and the earth,
and are reshaping their lives
in the search for justice and peace;
    let the people dance.

Dance, mountains and seas, office blocks and motorways, at the presence of the Lord.

A blessing on your good sense

1 Samuel 25.2–35

God of Abigail,
send us your blessing of good sense.
Send it where age-long feuds still fester
although no one remembers how they began.
Send it where people are sworn to seek revenge,
where judgement is distorted by jealousy
and where hatred has long buried humanity.

Send us your blessing of good sense
in the women and men of courage,
people with the vision of what might be
if once we trusted each other again.
Send us people who will walk ahead on the road
giving a lead in generosity and tolerance,
using all their powers of persuasion
to turn anger into forgiveness.

Send us your blessing of good sense
whenever we find ourselves afraid.
Send it to us as diplomats and politicians,
as employers and negotiators,
as spokespersons and go-betweens.
Send it to us in community associations,
in the council chamber and in parliament.

Send us your blessing of good sense
when our family is at odds,
when our neighbours fall out,
when our church is split,

94

when our nation is divided
and when the world totters on the verge of war.

Most wise God, whose gift of peace is beyond price, teach us the skills of peacemaking and fill our hearts with passion to practise them.

A high priest

Hebrews 6.13—7.3

What do we want with a high priest
in the succession of anyone?
The rituals of the Temple are past and gone
even among the Jews.
No animal is brought to sacrifice
and our devotion is expressed in our lives.
Christ Jesus is our saviour
and through him we are all priests to God.
But the priesthood of all believers
can too readily become the priesthood of no one;
and all these aspiring priests
belong to no succession and have no leader.

I dedicate myself to prayer.
Christ, whose prayers came from the heart,
whose prayers cost tears and agony,
be my high priest and teach me how to pray.

I dedicate myself to sacrifice.
Christ, you did not spare yourself
and you were generous even to your enemies,
be my high priest and teach me how to give.

I dedicate myself to reconciliation.
Christ, who broke down barriers
of gender, nation, wealth and power,
be my high priest and teach me integrity.

We thank you, God, for our high calling as priests in your
service, bringing the world into communion with you through
the grace of our great high priest who is Christ Jesus our Lord.

Lack of knowledge

Hosea 4.1–6

Both priest and prophet fail
for lack of knowledge and of the teaching of God.
We, who are both priests and prophets,
love all knowledge for the possibilities it has
of deepening our understanding of the living God.

You know the minds of children
are open to learn in countless ways;
help us as parents and teachers
to nourish them in all good things.

You know the potential for growth
you have given to every living soul;
help us as pupils and students
to increase our skills and information.

You know the endless possibilities
which lie before us as we learn;
help us as experimenters and researchers
to develop our knowledge for the good of all.

You know that we are pupils all our lives
through every moment until our dying hour;
help us to be open to new possibilities
and ready to learn from each other.

You know we confuse knowledge with facts,
and report with insight to the heart of things;
teach us to search after true wisdom
which reveals your nature and your purposes for us.

Married

Matthew 22.23–30

We choose not to keep the law of Moses
which secures the continuity of family
by making widows marry brothers-in-law.
We choose to take the possibility of divorce
in those same laws of Moses.
How, loving God and loving neighbour,
shall we pattern our lives as families
and as women and men in relationship?

We pray for the newly married, learning to live with each other and discovering uncomfortable truths about themselves as well as mutual love and strength.

We pray for new parents, filled with joy but also apprehension as they watch their growing child. May they learn to blend affection and discipline for their children's good.

We pray for young people, exploring their emotions and commitments to each other. May they find true friends and respect each others' dignity.

We pray for those seeking divorce and filled with a sense of failure, or anger or mutual blame. May it be a last resort when all else fails and not a hasty decision.

We pray for grandparents, aunts and uncles, and all the wider family circle who share the joys and pains of each other. May the bonds of love be strengthened between them.

God of the living, enrich the love we have for one another within your family.

Justice

Isaiah 11.1–5

Our justice is not God's justice;
we do the best we can to frame our laws,
to run our courts and prison service,
our police and other agencies,
impartially to serve the public good;
but we are human and our systems fail,
become corrupt or simply out of date.
We need renewal in the spirit of Christ.

Spirit of wisdom and understanding,
inform all those who frame the law
so that the poor may enjoy justice
and equity be a guiding principle.

Spirit of wisdom and understanding,
counsel all those who administer the law
so that our courts may be unbiased
and everyone have a fair hearing.

Spirit of wisdom and understanding,
direct those who enforce our laws
so that they enjoy our confidence
and people may go about their lives unafraid.

Spirit of wisdom and understanding,
enrich those who work with offenders
so that they may win their trust
and show them how to live in true community.

Spirit of wisdom and understanding,
redirect the lives of those who live by crime
so that they may find their fulfilment
in ways acceptable to everyone.

Spirit of wisdom and understanding, transform our human justice to make it more like yours.

From his mouth there went a sharp sword
Revelation 19.11–16

Faithful and True, Word of God,
King of kings and Lord of lords,
the one who has no name in any language we can speak
but was and is the Son of Man
bearing the new great name of love.

Teach us the value of words;
teach us to use them with care
so that they speak with meaning.

Take the babble of our words
which divide us in fear and misunderstanding
and make them a language of trust.

Take the child's first sounds
and shape them into words
full of innocence and love.

Take the meanness and poverty
of speech diluted with unmeant oaths
and make it speak of Christ with power.

Take the half-truths of propaganda,
the empty promises of vote-catchers
and the over-blown claims of advertisers
and show us what is worth our deepest hopes.

Take the words of conferences and committees
that fill the space between the walls

and let them burst out to make the things we do
more like our wisest plans.

Take us when we speak and make us messengers
of the Word which is faithful and true,
bringing the world justice and healing.

Teach us the value of words;
teach us to use them with care
so that they speak with meaning.

Staple wares
Ezekiel 27.12–24

The trade and commerce of ancient Tyre
is now reflected in every city high street;
goods from every corner of the earth
compete for our attention.
Our modest shopping trip means livelihoods
to people all around the world
and every worker in the store and supermarket.

As I make my choice of fruit and cheese,
search for sugar and count out tins;
as I select my coffee and breakfast cereals,
God give me pause for thought.

As I hunt for shoes and pick out socks,
look round the radios and kitchen-ware;
as I choose materials and knitting wool,
God give me pause for thought.

I pray for the growers and harvesters,
for the packers and export agents;
I pray for the food processors,
and the nimble fingers of the assembly line.
I pray, knowing my cheap goods
are someone else's low wage.
I pray, knowing I cannot opt out
of this market place of life
where I must make my choices.
I pray, seeking the good of everyone
on that long chain which leads from growers,

from manufacturers and agents
through the wholesalers and retailers
to my till receipt and carrier bag.
Help me to spend my wealth, which is not mine,
but your gift to us all, in the ways
which lead to prosperity for all your people.

The LORD is our righteousness

Jeremiah 23.5–8

Not only brought back from Egypt,
not only brought back from exile,
but brought back to wisdom, justice and righteousness.

We thought we knew where to find you,
we hardly needed a star to guide the way,
just perseverance and common sense;
why do you hide yourself away from the powerful
and join the refugees and outcasts,
calling us to follow you there?
Wise God, give us wisdom.

We thought we had laid you safe in the manger;
we wrapped you in the thickest sentiment we could find,
and stressed how long ago you came to us;
why do you break upon us in our daily life
with messages of peace and goodwill,
demanding that we do something about it?
Just and righteous God, give us justice and righteousness.

You are the God who made childless Sarah laugh;
you took cheating Jacob to father a nation;
Moses, from the household of Pharaoh, became a deliverer;
the despised Jeremiah was right in the end.
The weakness of Esther and Rahab and Miriam
was turned into power when your moment came.
You scattered your people in Assyria and Babylon,
where they learnt the greatness of your love;
out of what seemed chaos and disaster

your wisdom, justice and righteousness prevailed.
So where else would we expect to find you
but in the ordinary place with the faithful people,
turning the world to your purpose through them?
Bring us to that manger, to that true rejoicing,
which will make wisdom, justice and righteousness alive
in us.

Holy, holy, holy

Revelation 4

Sophisticated people do not believe
in a God of lightning flashes and thunder,
on a throne surrounded by fabulous beasts.
Sophisticated people need no pictures;
they see God in pure imagination
and yet, somehow, sophisticated people
begin to lose the art of worship.

Holy, holy, holy God,
beyond our sight and understanding,
found in the pure light which blinds our eyes;
understood when all mysteries are made plain;
we worship and adore you.

Holy, holy, holy God,
whose great power is revealed in great mercy,
hear our prayers and look on us with kindness.
We have seen your love in Christ Jesus;
we worship and adore you.

Holy, holy, holy God,
whose presence is everywhere,
enlivening our praise and service
whenever we offer ourselves in faith.
We worship and adore you.

Glorious Trinity, life-giving and sustaining, the source of all our
happiness, we come into your awesome presence through the
grace of Christ Jesus, Emmanuel.

Further Titles from SPCK
AVAILABLE NOW

Making Holy Dreams Come True
A book of prayers and meditations

By Garth Hewitt
Photographs by Wilf Whitty

An imaginatively illustrated book of seasonal prayers, daily prayers and prayers for special occasions relating particularly to the work of the Amos Trust, which has projects in four parts of the world: in South Africa with street children; in Nicaragua with education among poor communities; in Israel/Palestine supporting peace and reconciliation projects, and in India working with a Dalit community.

As we grapple with the joys and challenges of everyday living, it's not always easy to trust in the sustaining power and love of God who is always so ready to meet us. With its invigorating, vividly illustrated meditations, *Making Holy Dreams Come True* aims to help us deepen our faith as we think through how we relate to God and to the world around us. Offering daily prayers, prayers that draw our attention to particular situations overseas, seasonal prayers and prayers for special occasions, this richly rewarding book is primarily for personal use, although it may also be used in communal settings.

Price: £12.99

ISBN-13: 9780281058570
ISBN-10: 0281058571

Further Titles from SPCK
AVAILABLE NOW

Rumours of Life
Transforming wounded people

By David Runcorn

Grief-stricken and bereft, the first disciples were in no fit state to take on board the astonishing idea that Jesus had risen from the dead. When we explore the strange cluster of stories describing the resurrection appearances, we may have much sympathy for them! And yet we cannot help but be moved by the infinite care with which Jesus reaches out to these individuals, as, through unexpected ways and meetings, he transforms a broken, dispirited and unbelieving community into a living Church.

Rumours of Life reminds us that the truly real is truly mysterious. It offers deep reassurance that, however difficult or confusing our present circumstances, we can have hope. For God raised Jesus Christ from the dead, and we are never alone on our personal journey to new birth in him.

David Runcorn is or has been an accordionist, vicar, fast bowler and hermit. He was until recently Principal of Trinity College, Bristol, and is now director of Ministry Development in the Lichfield Diocese.

Price: £8.99

ISBN-13: 9780281058693
ISBN-10: 0281058695